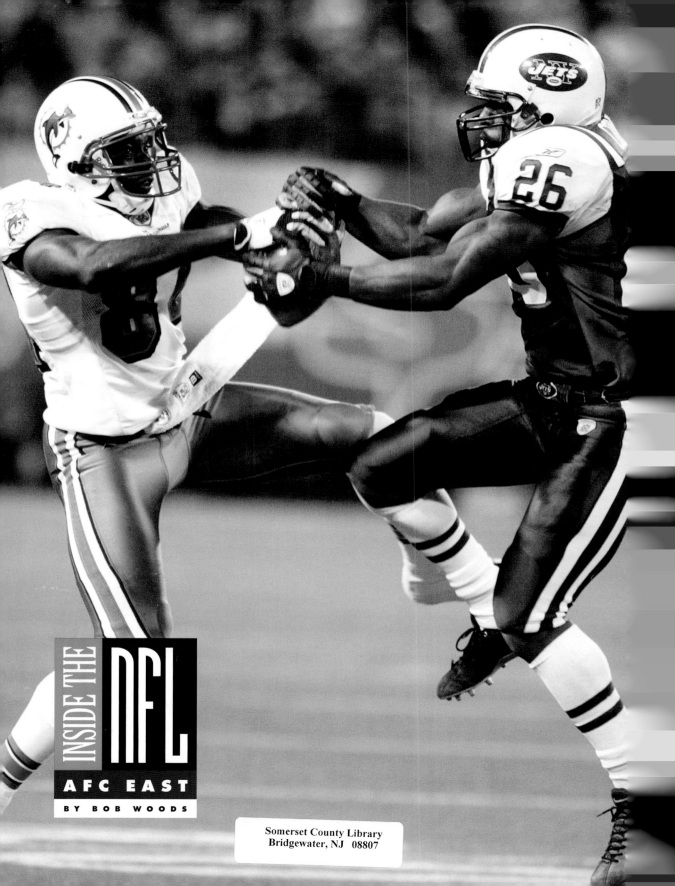

INSIDE THE NFL
AFC EAST
BY BOB WOODS

LIBRARY OF CONGRESS CATALOGING-IN-PUBLICATION DATA

Woods, Bob.
  AFC East / by Bob Woods.
    p. cm. — (Inside the NFL)
  Includes index.
  ISBN 1-59296-508-3 (library bound : alk. paper) 1. National Football
League—History—Juvenile literature. 2. Football—United States—History—Juvenile
literature. I. Title: American Football Conference East. II. Title. III. Child's World of
sports. Inside the NFL.
  GV955.5.N35W65 2006
  796.332'64'0973—dc22   2005004810

ACKNOWLEDGEMENTS

The Child's World®: Mary Berendes, Publishing Director

Editorial Directions, Inc.: Russell Primm, Editorial Director and Line Editor; Matt
Messbarger, Project Editor; Elizabeth K. Martin, Assistant Editor; Olivia Nellums,
Editorial Assistant; Susan Hindman, Copy Editor; Susan Ashley, Beth Franken,
Proofreaders; Kevin Cunningham, Fact Checker; Tim Griffin/IndexServ, Indexer;
James Buckley Jr., Photo Researcher and Selector

The Design Lab: Kathleen Petelinsek, Design and Page Production

Photos: Cover: Stephan Savoia/AP
AP: 16; Al Bello/Getty: 38; Bruce Bennett Studios/Getty: 27; Bettmann/Corbis: 25;
David Drapkin/Getty: 2; Tom Hauck/Allsport/Getty: 37; Ann Heisenfelt/AP: 32; Don
Heupel/AP: 14; Doug Mills/AP: 30; Mike Powell/Allsport/Getty: 28; Kevin Rivoli/AP:
11; Stephan Savoia/AP: 42; Roberto Schmidt/AFP/Getty: 21; Paul Spinelli/Getty: 23,
41; Sports Gallery/Al Messerschmidt: 7, 10, 12, 18, 20, 26, 35; Shannon Stapleton/
Reuters/Corbis: 1; Rick Stewart/Allsport/Getty: 8; Rick Stewart/Getty; 19, 36

A F C E A S T

TABLE OF CONTENTS

Published in the United States of America by
The Child's World® • PO Box 326
Chanhassen, MN 55317-0326
800-599-READ • www.childsworld.com

The
Child's
World

INTRODUCTION

BUFFALO BILLS

Year Founded: 1960

**Home Stadium:
Ralph Wilson
Stadium**

**Year Stadium
Opened: 1973**

**Team Colors: Red
and blue**

MIAMI DOLPHINS

Year Founded: 1966

**Home Stadium: Pro
Player Stadium**

**Year Stadium
Opened: 1987**

**Team Colors: Aqua,
coral, and blue**

The National Football League (NFL) was founded in Canton, Ohio, in 1920. Its original name was the American Professional Football Association, which was changed to the NFL in 1922. At first, there were 14 teams, with names such as the Akron Pros, the Rochester Jeffersons, and the Muncie Flyers.

In 1960, a competing group of eight teams called the American Football League (AFL) was launched. The two leagues agreed in 1966 to **merge,** beginning with the 1970 season. Following the 1966 season, however, the two leagues' champs played the first AFL-NFL World Championship Game. That historic contest, in which the NFL-champion Green Bay Packers trounced the AFL-champion Kansas City Chiefs, 35–10, is now known as Super Bowl I.

For the 1969 season, the NFL had 16 teams, and the AFL had 10. By 1970, when the two leagues merged, there were 26 teams. Now called the NFL, the league was divided again into the National Football Conference and the American Football Conference. The NFL has since expanded to 32 teams, with four four-team divisions in each conference. The **franchises** that make up the AFC East are the Buffalo Bills, the Miami Dolphins, the New England Patriots, and the New York Jets.

Three of those teams were original members of the AFL, yet each one has achieved remarkable "firsts" in NFL history. The Bills claim the league's first player to rush for 2,000 yards in a single season (O.J. Simpson, 1973). The 1972 Dolphins remain the NFL's first and only "perfect" team. They won all 14 regular-season games, two playoff games, and Super Bowl VII. The Patriots capped a dramatic 2001 season, which they started 5–5, by becoming the first team to win a Super Bowl on the final play.

The Jets' "first" remains one of the most stunning moments in sports history. They made it all the way to Super Bowl III. New York's brash young quarterback, Joe Namath, predicted a victory over the 18-point-favorite Baltimore Colts. Namath and the Jets made good on the promise, winning 16–7 and becoming the first AFL victor in the Super Bowl.

Namath is just one of several outstanding AFC East quarterbacks, from Bob Griese and Jack Kemp in the old AFL days to current stars Tom Brady and Chad Pennington. In the chapters ahead, you'll read about them, plus many other exciting players who have made this division so entertaining.

NEW ENGLAND PATRIOTS*

Year Founded: 1960

Home Stadium: Gillette Stadium

Year Stadium Opened: 2002

Team Colors: Red, silver, and blue

* *Boston Patriots until 1971*

NEW YORK JETS**

Year Founded: 1960

Home Stadium: Giants Stadium

Year Stadium Opened: 1976

Team Colors: Green and white

***New York Titans until 1963*

CHAPTER ONE

THE BUFFALO BILLS

Buffalo, New York, is famous for its hot and spicy chicken wings and cold and snowy winters. Fans go through plenty of both at Ralph Wilson Stadium, where their hometown Bills play a rough and tumble brand of NFL football.

Like their wings and winters, the Bills have been hot and cold over the years. The team spent its first 10 seasons in the old AFL. They suffered losing records in 1960 and 1961, then finished 7–6–1 in 1962. The Bills had the same record in 1963, but went to the AFL playoffs for the first time. There they lost to the Patriots, 26–8.

Those Bills featured two stars on offense: quarterback Jack Kemp and rugged fullback Carlton "Cookie" Gilchrist. They also boasted the AFL's best defense, led by tackle Tom Sestak. Everything came together in 1964, when Buffalo captured its first AFL Eastern Division title with a 12–2 record. They went on to win the AFL Championship, defeating the San Diego Chargers, 20–7. The Bills were champs again

Although the New York Jets and New York Giants have New York in their names, only the Bills actually play in New York State. Both the Jets and Giants play in Giants Stadium, which is in Rutherford, New Jersey.

Future U.S. Congressman Jack Kemp led the Bills in the 1960s.

in 1965, shutting out the Chargers in the title game, 23–0.

Still hot enough to win a third straight division title, Buffalo cooled off in the 1966 AFL Championship game, falling to the Kansas City Chiefs. Then the Bills went into a deep freeze for six miserable seasons, winning 17 games, losing 64, and tying 3. A bright spot came when they drafted **Heisman Trophy** winner Orenthal James "O.J." Simpson in 1969.

Jim Kelly helped take the Bills to four consecutive Super Bowls.

In 1973, the Bills moved into Rich Stadium (renamed Ralph Wilson Stadium in 1998), while Simpson moved into the NFL record books by rushing for 2,003 yards. That triggered the first of three winning seasons, after which Buffalo shuffled off into another hibernation. Future Hall of Famer Simpson lost his punch, too. "The Juice" was traded to the San Francisco 49ers in 1978.

The Bills awoke from their slumber in 1980, winning their first division title in 14 years. They met their **nemesis,** the Chargers, in the playoffs and lost, 20–14. Running back Joe Cribbs's 1,097 yards rushing boosted the Bills to a **wild-card** spot in the 1981 playoffs. They winged the Jets, 31–27, for their first playoff triumph since 1965. However, the following week against the Cincinnati Bengals, their season ended with a 28–21 loss.

The Bills stayed in the losing mode for the next six seasons. The club finished below .500 every year except 1983, when they broke even at 8–8. Marv Levy took over as head coach during the 1986 season, and faithful fans would soon be frolicking again.

Paced by quarterback Jim Kelly and running back Thurman Thomas, Levy created a brilliant **no-huddle offense.** The Bills won the AFC East in 1988, but lost

In 1999, former Bills guard Billy Shaw became the first player who spent his entire career in the AFL to be inducted into the Pro Football Hall of Fame.

Thurman Thomas could catch the ball as well as he could run with it.

Former Bills coach Marv Levy is a member of the Phi Beta Kappa honor society and earned his master's degree in English history from Harvard.

to the Bengals in the conference championship game. Atop the East again in 1989, they dropped their first playoff game to the Cleveland Browns.

The next season would be a special one for Buffalo and its loyal fans. The no-huddle offense was humming. The defense, powered by defensive end Bruce Smith and linebacker Cornelius Bennett,

Defensive end Bruce Smith was a fearsome sight to opposing quarterbacks.

The arrival of Drew Bledsoe in 2002 meant a new era in Buffalo.

throttled opponents. The Bills ended up with a franchise-best 13–3 record. After getting by the Miami Dolphins in the divisional play-off game, they riddled the Oakland Raiders, 51–3. The Bills finally reached the Super Bowl!

Super Bowl XXV turned out to be one of the most exciting ever. The game matched the Bills' offensive **juggernaut** against the New York Giants' stingy defense. Yet New York's ball-control offense slowed Kelly and company. The Giants kept the ball for more than 40 of the game's 60 minutes. Still, with four seconds remaining and the Giants leading 20–19, the Bills had a chance to win. As all of western New York State held its breath, kicker Scott Norwood's 47-yard field goal attempt sailed wide right.

Incredibly, the Bills made it to the next three Super Bowls. Just as incredibly, they came up short all three times. They would make four more trips to the playoffs during the 1990s, but failed to reach the Super Bowl. Regardless, Buffalo completed the decade with an AFC-best record of 103–57.

The new millennium found the franchise right back in the **postseason.** It appeared as if the Bills would win the wild-card game against the Tennessee Titans, until a bizarre kickoff return for a touchdown with three seconds left doomed Buffalo. In 2002, a trade with the Patriots brought superstar quarterback Drew Bledsoe to town. The team finished 8–8, but Bledsoe set a franchise record, passing for 4,359 yards.

After the Bills stumbled to a 6–10 record in 2003, third-year head coach Gregg Williams was replaced by Mike Mularkey, the former offensive coordinator in Pittsburgh. Things didn't look like they would be any better in 2004, when the Bills lost five of their first six games. But they rebounded to win eight of their next nine

In the 1992 wild-card playoff game against the Houston Oilers, Buffalo rallied from being behind by 32 points in the third quarter to win 41–38—the largest comeback in NFL history.

Willis McGahee gives the Bills some muscle in the backfield.

Bills quarter-
back Jack Kemp
(1962–1969) went
on to serve in the
U.S. Congress from
1971–1989, and
ran for president
in 1988.

while playing some of the best football in the league. That stretch, plus the emergence of second-year back Willis McGahee as a top runner, left Bills fans excited for 2005—because, while chicken wings and snow-storms remain part of life in Buffalo, so, too, does Bills football.

CHAPTER TWO

THE MIAMI DOLPHINS

"The dolphin is one of the fastest and smartest creatures of the sea," said Joe Robbie, owner of the AFL's first expansion team, in announcing its name on October 8, 1965. The Miami Dolphins would **debut** less than a year later, and *fast* and *smart* pretty well described the new team. Their speedy running back Joe Auer returned the very first opening kickoff 95 yards for a touchdown—though the Oakland Raiders rallied and won, 23–14.

Miami didn't taste victory until its sixth game, beating the Denver Broncos in the Orange Bowl, and won only twice more that inaugural season. The team "improved" to 4–10 the following year, yet better times were approaching. The franchise drafted wisely. In the next three years, they chose quarterback Bob Griese, running backs Larry Csonka and Jim Kiick, and guard Larry Little. Don Shula replaced George Wilson as head coach in 1970. Then "the Fins"—as the team is sometimes called (even though dolphins are really mammals)—really started swimming.

On Christmas Day 1971, the Dolphins won the longest game (82 minutes, 40 seconds) in pro football history, 27–24, at Kansas City. Miami's Garo Yepremian kicked a 37-yard field goal in the second overtime of the AFC semifinal playoff game.

Bruising fullback Larry Csonka was the star of Super Bowl VIII.

Players at the Dolphins' first training camp in 1966 complained they couldn't sleep at night: the seals at nearby Sea World were barking too much!

The 1970 Dolphins won six games in a row, down the stretch. Their 10–4 record earned them their first trip to the playoffs. They lost to the Raiders, 21–14, but they'd be back. Indeed, Miami captured its first AFC Eastern Division title in 1971. Their great play continued in the postseason. By beating the Chiefs and then the Baltimore Colts, they won a trip to Super Bowl VI against the Dallas Cowboys. The

Dolphins chose a bad time to play their worst game of the season, losing 24–3.

There would be no losing for the 1972 Dolphins, however. In the greatest NFL season ever for a team, Miami went undefeated. Their perfect 14–0 record lasted through the playoffs, with wins over Cleveland and Pittsburgh. The Dolphins completed their 17–0 season with a 14–7 victory over the Washington Redskins in Super Bowl VII.

The Dolphins lost twice in 1973, yet won their third straight AFC East championship and fourth consecutive trip to the postseason. Csonka rushed for 117 yards and three touchdowns in Miami's 27–10 romp over the Raiders in the AFC title game. Then, in the Super Bowl VIII **demolition** of the Minnesota Vikings (24–7), Csonka ran for a record 145 yards and a pair of touchdowns. "Dol-fans" had witnessed the best two-year run in NFL history, at 32–2.

The trio of Csonka, Kiick, and star receiver Paul Warfield left the team to join the new World Football League in 1975. The Dolphins squad still managed an 11–3 record that season, but lost in the playoffs.

They didn't always win it all, but Shula's teams remained a force in the AFC East. They returned to the playoffs in 1978 and 1979. In the 1979 season, old hero Csonka came back for his grand finale, and the Dolphins won their first division title since 1974.

The Fins waltzed back to the Big Dance in the strike-shortened 1982 season, finishing 7–2 and earning a wild-card berth.

Five other quarterbacks were selected ahead of Dan Marino in the 1983 NFL draft: John Elway (Colts), Jim Kelly (Bills), Tony Eason (Patriots), Ken O'Brien (Jets), and Todd Blackledge (Chiefs).

Miami couldn't stop Washington's John Riggins in Super Bowl XVII.

Featuring the "Killer Bees" defense (six players' names started with the letter B), they beat the Patriots, Chargers, and Jets in the play-offs. Their run ended in Super Bowl XVII, however, as the Redskins prevailed, 27–17.

The franchise made its smartest move in 1983 by drafting University of Pittsburgh quarterback Dan Marino. Not only would Marino lead the Dolphins to another division title in his rookie season, but he went on to throw more passes (8,358) for more completions (4,967), more yards (61,361), and more touchdowns (420) than any player in NFL history.

Amazingly, while Miami qualified for the post-season in 10 of Marino's 17 years with the club, they only went to one Super Bowl. That was in 1984, when Marino tossed an NFL-record 48 touchdown passes in the regular season. He had eight more in the play-offs. Unfortunately, in the Super Bowl the 49ers held

Dan Marino passed for at least one touchdown in 30 consecutive games from 1985 to 1987. Only the Colts' John Unitas (47 games) and the Packers' Brett Favre (36) ever had longer streaks.

Dan Marino is the most prolific passer in NFL history.

Mark Duper, Mark Clayton, and Dan Marino before Super Bowl XIX.

On another historic Christmas Day, in 1994, Don Shula won the 319th regular-season game of his career, surpassing the Chicago Bears' George Halas for the all-time record for most career regular-season wins by an NFL

off Marino and the "Marks Brothers," wide receivers Mark Clayton and Mark Duper. The Dolphins lost Super Bowl XIX, 38–16.

Shula retired after the 1995 season, and Marino departed following the 1999 season. Dave Wannstedt took over as head coach for Jimmy Johnson in 2000. The team reached the playoffs that season, led by running back Lamar Smith. Miami won a thrilling comeback game, 23–17 in overtime, against the Colts in the playoffs. However, the Raiders shut the Fins

This dramatic run by Lamar Smith carried Miami past the Colts in the 2000 playoffs.

In 2002, Ricky Williams became the first Dolphins player to lead the league in rushing.

out a week later. In 2001, Miami made the playoffs with an 11–5 record, but were bumped off this time by the Baltimore Ravens in the first round.

A wise trade brought running back Ricky Williams to Miami in 2002. The 1998 Heisman Trophy winner led the NFL in rushing yards (1,853) and ran for 16 touchdowns. The Dolphins just missed going to the postseason that year and again the next, falling short only on tiebreakers each time.

In 2004, though, the franchise's fortunes took a sudden turn for the worse. Williams abruptly retired shortly before the start of the season, and the Dolphins had no one to turn to on offense. Only the efforts of the defensive standouts such as linebacker Zach Thomas and defensive end Jason Taylor kept a 4–12 season from being any poorer. Wannstedt retired midway through the season, and the Dolphins hired college coach Nick Saban, who led LSU to a national title in 2003, as head coach for 2005.

The Dolphins may have been down in 2004. But with their fast and smart tradition, they're sure to make another splash before long.

End Jason Taylor is a star on the Dolphins' defense.

CHAPTER THREE

THE NEW ENGLAND PATRIOTS

A Boston news-paper contest was held in 1959 to choose a name for the city's new football team. Thousands of entries were submitted, and 74 fans suggested the winning moniker, the Patriots.

Billy Sullivan was awarded the eighth and final franchise in the new AFL in 1959. Soon after, the owner selected "Pat Patriot," a minuteman, for the team **logo.** "Patient Pat" might have been more appropriate. As the team and its fans would learn, good things come to those who wait.

The Boston Patriots—as the team was initially called—met the Denver Broncos in the very first AFL regular-season game, on September 9, 1960. They lost, 13–10, and finished the year with a 5–9 record.

In the **off-season,** Boston traded for veteran quarterback Babe Parilli. They also switched cornerback Gino Cappelletti to wide receiver. The moves paid off, as the team improved to 9–4–1 in each of the next two seasons. In 1963, they tied the Bills for the division lead, at 7–6–1. The game to decide the title, played in Buffalo's snow-filled War Memorial Stadium, went the Pats' way. Yet they were trounced in the AFL Championship Game by the Chargers, 51–10.

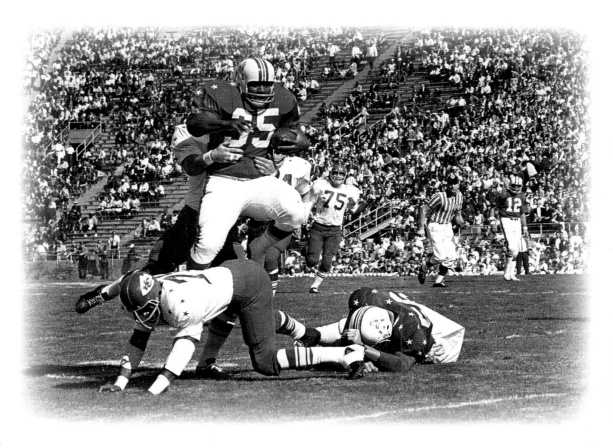

Jim Nance (No. 35) was a star runner for the Patriots in their early seasons.

The Patriots had talent in those early years. The draft produced linebacker Nick Buoniconti and fullback Jim Nance. A solid defense featured linemen Houston Antwine, Bob Dee, Larry Eisenhauer, and Jim Lee Hunt, plus center Jon Morris. What they lacked was enough offense to keep them in contention.

They also were without a permanent home for their first 11 seasons. The Patriots played at Boston University Field in 1960 and 1961 and at Harvard in 1962 and again in 1970. From 1963 to 1969,

Schaefer Stadium was renamed Sullivan Stadium on May 23, 1983, in honor of the Patriots' founder, William H. "Billy" Sullivan Sr. The Pats' current home, Gillette Stadium, was originally named CMGI Field.

Jim Plunkett was drafted first overall in 1971 by the Patriots.

they called plays in Fenway Park, usually home to baseball's Red Sox. Finally, in 1971, the Pats took up full-time residence in new Schaefer Stadium in Foxboro, about 25 miles (40 kilometers) south of Boston. They changed their name, too, becoming the New England Patriots.

A fresh crop of players came aboard over the next several years. The franchise drafted Stanford's Heisman Trophy quarterback Jim Plunkett in 1971.

Jim Plunkett was the first of three consecutive quarterbacks selected at the top of the 1971 draft. Archie Manning (to the Saints) and Dan Pastorini (Oilers) followed him.

Running back Sam Cunningham (diving for a touchdown) and guard John Hannah (No. 73) are two of the greatest players in Patriots history.

A strong running game and a stingy defense carried the Patriots to Super Bowl XX in the 1985 season.

Two years later, they picked fullback Sam "Bam" Cunningham, wide receiver Darryl Stingley, and guard John Hannah. The team went 7–7 in 1974.

Plunkett was traded to the 49ers after the 1975 season. The team responded in 1976 with its best season to date, going 11–3. A six-game winning streak propelled New England to its second-ever playoff appearance. The bubble burst in the wild-card game versus the Oakland Raiders, with a heartbreaking 24–21 loss in the final seconds.

The Patriots captured the division title in 1978, despite the loss of Stingley after a devastating hit left him paralyzed. They then dropped their playoff game to the Houston Oilers. Following a dismal 2–14 season in 1981, New England returned to the postseason, only to lose to Miami.

In 1985, second-year head coach Raymond Berry took the 11–5 Patriots all the way to Super Bowl XX. That memorable season screeched to a halt, however, when the Chicago Bears devoured them, 46–10.

After another playoff appearance in 1986, New England endured a long dry spell. The team hit rock bottom in 1990, going 1–15. Hope arrived in 1993 when Bill Parcells, who

The Patriots beat the Dolphins 3–0 in the famous "Snow-Plow Game" of 1982. A snow-plow operator cleared a path for the game-winning field goal in the fourth quarter.

Quarterback Tom Brady was the Most Valuable Player (MVP) of the Patriots' wins in Super Bowls XXXVI and XXXVIII.

Quarterback Tom Brady went to the same Bay Area high school (Serra High in San Mateo, California) that also produced baseball star Barry Bonds.

had guided the New York Giants to Super Bowl wins in 1986 and 1990, became head coach. The Pats were 5–11 that year, but a potent offense was emerging around quarterback Drew Bledsoe.

New England made the playoffs in 1994 and 1996. With the additions of running back Curtis Martin and wide receiver Terry Glenn, the 1996 squad bulled its way to Super Bowl XXXI. Unfortunately, they encountered another NFC powerhouse, this time the Green Bay Packers, who won the game, 35–21.

The Patriots enjoyed moderate success from then until the magical 2001 season. That year, under head coach Bill Belichick, New England was 5–5 with six games remaining. Bledsoe had suffered an injury in the second game. Inexperienced backup Tom Brady took the reins. The Pats finished with a six-game winning streak to reach the playoffs.

Wild describes New England's 16–13 overtime victory against the Raiders. The game was played in a blinding snowstorm at Foxboro Stadium. Following a controversial reversal of an apparent Brady fumble, Patriots kicker Adam Vinatieri connected on the tying field goal, and the Patriots won in overtime.

The Pats beat the Steelers in the AFC title game, then met the heavily favored St. Louis Rams in Super Bowl XXXVI. New England led 17–3 after three quarters, then the Rams' high-octane offense tied the game with 90 seconds left. Brady, with no time outs, marched his troops to the Rams' 30-yard line. Vinatieri lined up for a 48-yard field goal as time expired and . . . Pats win! Pats win!

Many football fans dismissed the upset win over the Rams as a fluke. Instead, it was a hint of things to come. Indeed, what the Packers were to the 1960s, the Steelers to the '70s, the 49ers to the '80s, and the Cowboys to the '90s, the Patriots are to the 2000s.

After missing the playoffs on a tiebreaker in a 9–7 season in 2002, New England was back on top in 2003. The Patriots won their

**Marvin Harrison's (No. 37) late interception sealed New England's
24–21 victory over Philadelphia in Super Bowl XXXIX.**

last 15 games of the season, including a 32–29 victory over Carolina
in Super Bowl XXXVIII when Vinatieri kicked another game winner.

In 2004, the Patriots won 14 regular-season games again, then
cruised past excellent Indianapolis and Pittsburgh teams in the playoffs.
Finally, after their team's 24–21 victory over the Eagles in Super Bowl
XXXIX, New England fans had a certifiable dynasty on their hands.
With their third Super Bowl win in four seasons, the Patriots have taken
their place alongside some of the greatest teams in NFL history.

CHAPTER FOUR

THE NEW YORK JETS

Beginning in the early 1990s, a fan started wearing a green and white firefighter's helmet to Jets games. On the shoulders of another fan, he led a rousing cheer at home games: "J-E-T-S, Jets, Jets, Jets!" If things had gone differently 30 years earlier, he would be shouting: "T-I-T-A-N-S, Titans, Titans, Titans!" New York definitely wouldn't be the same without their beloved J-E-T-S.

The franchise was originally dubbed the New York Titans by its first owner, Harry Wismer. Maybe he should have gone with the name Titanic instead. While the team did well enough during its first three seasons, off the field it was a sinking ship.

> The Titans' team colors were blue and gold.

The Titans played home games at the Polo Grounds. The New York Giants baseball team played there before moving to San Francisco in 1958. Behind a strong passing game, the Titans went 7–7 in each of their first two years. Their star was future Hall of Fame receiver Don Maynard. In 1962, they dropped to 5–9.

Meanwhile, Wismer argued with his players, AFL Commissioner Joe Foss, and the New York media. The team's finances were a mess, too.

By the end of the 1962 season, Wismer was **bankrupt.** He sold the franchise to Sonny Werblin for $1 million. Werblin changed the team's name to the Jets and hired head coach Weeb Ewbank. Ewbank had led the Baltimore Colts to NFL championships in 1958 and 1959. In 1964, the Jets moved into brand-new Shea Stadium.

The club finished a disappointing 5–8–1 in each of Ewbank's first three seasons. But in 1965, they drafted University of Alabama quarterback Joe Namath, who eventually would take them to the promised land. The team finally put together a winning season in 1967, finishing 8–5–1. Namath became the first quarterback to throw for more than 4,000 yards in a season, and fans flocked to sold-out Shea.

They were rewarded a year later when the Jets improved to 11–3. Thirteen Jets were named to the AFL All-Star team. New York knocked off Oakland in the AFL Championship Game, 27–23. Next came a trip to Miami for Super Bowl III.

Their opponents were the mighty Colts, who the "experts" swore would crush the Jets. A confident Namath, however, boldly "guaranteed" a New York victory. Usually in sports, bold guarantees have a way of coming back to haunt you. However, in true David-versus-Goliath fashion, "Broadway Joe" backed up his words. The Jets shocked everyone, winning 16–7. Some people now call it the biggest upset in NFL history.

The Jets went to the playoffs again in 1969, but lost to Kansas City. New York kicked off the inaugural year of the AFL-NFL merger

Flamboyant quarterback Joe Namath was a star on and off the field.

in 1970 by playing in the first-ever *Monday Night Football* game, which the Cleveland Browns won, 31–21. From there, the Jets went into a tailspin to 4–10.

In fact, the team would not finish a season above .500 until 1981. Sparked by a sack-happy defense, starring Mark Gastineau and Joe Klecko,

Joe Namath was also selected in the first round (12th overall) of the 1965 NFL draft by the St. Louis Cardinals.

the Jets went 10–5–1 that year. They advanced to the playoffs for the first time since 1969, but lost to the Bills. They posted a 6–3 record in 1982, and won two playoff games before being shut out by the Dolphins, 14–0, in the AFC Championship Game.

The Jets appeared in the postseason in 1985 and 1986, dropping the wild-card once in 1985. In 1991, an 8–8 record was good enough for a wild-card berth.

Defensive end Mark Gastineau anchored the "New York Sack Exchange" of the 1980s.

Wide receiver Keyshawn Johnson and the Jets made it
to the AFC title game in 1998, but lost to the Broncos.

They bombed again, this time slipping to the Oilers.

The Jets were grounded from then until 1997. That's when football's white knight, Bill Parcells, rode back into Giants Stadium. That was the Jets' home field, which they had been sharing with their cross-town rivals since 1984. Parcells instantly lifted a team that had lost 33 of its previous 37 games.

Weeb Ewbank was the only coach to lead teams to championships in both the AFL (the Jets) and the NFL (the Colts).

Curtis Martin is the Jets' all-time leading rusher.

By 1998, the Jets were 12–4 and won their first AFC East championship. Led by quarterback Vinny Testaverde, the Jets knocked off the Jacksonville Jaguars in the playoffs. Running back Curtis Martin and wide receiver Keyshawn Johnson each scored two touchdowns. In the AFC Championship Game, New York held a 10–0 third-quarter lead over Denver. However, the Broncos rallied and won, 23–10.

Testaverde ruptured his **Achilles tendon** in the opening game of the 1999 season and was out for the year. Still, the Jets, who started out 1–6, ended at 8–8. The highlight of the 2000 season (9–7) was a wild fourth-quarter rally against the Dolphins. New York trailed by 23 points, but came back to win 40–37 in overtime.

The Jets had four first-round draft choices in 2000 and they selected four future starters: defensive ends Shaun Ellis and John Abraham, quarterback Chad Pennington, and tight end Anthony Becht.

In 2001, Herman Edwards took over as head coach. The Jets' John Hall kicked a game-winning field goal in the season finale against the Raiders, sending the Jets to the playoffs. But they lost to those same Raiders in the wild-card game. Oakland ended another improbable Jets postseason run in 2002.

Behind 22-year-old quarterback sensation Chad Pennington, New York won the AFC East with a 9–7 record. In the playoffs, they shut out the Colts, 41–0, then fell to the Raiders.

With Pennington injured much of the following season, the Jets won only six games in 2003. But they bounced back in 2004 with a memorable season.

New York bolted out of the gate that year with five straight wins and went on to finish 10–6, earning a wild-card playoff berth. Pennington passed for 16 touchdowns and Martin, at the age of 31, ran for 1,697 yards to become the oldest player ever to win an NFL rushing title. On defense, ends Shaun Ellis and John Abraham anchored a stingy unit that ranked among the best in club history.

Then, in the wild-card game at AFC West-champion San Diego, the Jets pulled out a stirring victory, winning 20–17 in overtime on Doug Brien's field goal. The next week, the Jets traveled to Pittsburgh to face a Steelers team that was riding a 14-game winning streak. They battled the heavily favored Steelers to another overtime, but this time New York was on the wrong end of a deciding field goal. Pittsburgh won 20–17.

Still, three playoff appearances in four seasons spell good things ahead for the J-E-T-S.

Quarterback Chad Pennington is known for his poise on the field.

STAT STUFF

T E A M   R E C O R D S

TEAM	ALL-TIME RECORD	NFL TITLES (MOST RECENT)	NUMBER OF TIMES IN PLAYOFFS	TOP COACH (WINS)
Buffalo	322–346–8	2* (1965)	17	Marv Levy (123)
Miami	**353–235–4**	**2 (1973)**	**21**	**Don Shula (274)**
New England	328–339–9	3 (2004)	14	Bill Belichick (62)
New York	**304–364–8**	**1* (1968)**	**11**	**Weeb Ewbank (73)**

(*AFL championships)

The Patriots and wide receiver Deion Branch, the Super Bowl XXXIX MVP, were champions again in 2004.

MORE STAT STUFF

MEMBERS OF THE PRO FOOTBALL HALL OF FAME

BUFFALO PLAYER	POSITION	DATE INDUCTED
Joe DeLamielleure	Guard	2003
Jim Kelly	Quarterback	2002
Marv Levy	Coach	2001
James Lofton	Wide Receiver	2003
Billy Shaw	Guard	1999
O. J. Simpson	Running back	1985

NEW ENGLAND PLAYER	POSITION	DATE INDUCTED
Nick Buoniconti	Linebacker	2001
John Hannah	Guard	1991
Mike Haynes	Cornerback	1997

MIAMI PLAYER	POSITION	DATE INDUCTED
Nick Buoniconti	Linebacker	2001
Larry Csonka	Running back	1987
Bob Griese	Quarterback	1990
Jim Langer	Center	1987
Larry Little	Guard	1993
Dan Marino	Quarterback	2005
Don Shula	Coach	1997
Dwight Stephenson	Center	1998
Paul Warfield	Wide receiver	1983

NEW YORK PLAYER	POSITION	DATE INDUCTED
Weeb Ewbank	Coach	1978
Ronnie Lott	Cornerback/Safety	2000
Don Maynard	Wide receiver	1987
Joe Namath	Quarterback	1985
John Riggins	Running back	1992

MORE STAT STUFF

A F C   E A S T   C A R E E R   L E A D E R S   (T H R O U G H   2 0 0 4)

BUFFALO

CATEGORY	NAME (YEARS WITH TEAM)	TOTAL
Rushing yards	Thurman Thomas (1988-1999)	11,938
Passing yards	Jim Kelly (1986-1996)	35,467
Touchdown passes	Jim Kelly (1986-1996)	237
Receptions	Andre Reed (1985-1999)	941
Touchdowns	Andre Reed (1985-1999)	87
Scoring	Steve Christie (1992-2000)	1,011

MIAMI

CATEGORY	NAME (YEARS WITH TEAM)	TOTAL
Rushing yards	Larry Csonka (1968-1974, 1979)	6,737
Passing yards	Dan Marino (1983-1999)	61,361
Touchdown passes	Dan Marino (1983-1999)	420
Receptions	Mark Clayton (1983-1992)	550
Touchdowns	Mark Clayton (1983-1992)	82
Scoring	Olindo Mare (1997-2004)	840

NEW ENGLAND

CATEGORY	NAME (YEARS WITH TEAM)	TOTAL
Rushing yards	Sam Cunningham (1973-79, 1981-82)	5,453
Passing yards	Drew Bledsoe (1993-2001)	29,657
Touchdown passes	Steve Grogan (1975-1990)	182
Receptions	Stanley Morgan (1977-1989)	534
Touchdowns	Stanley Morgan (1977-1989)	68
Scoring	Gino Cappelletti (1960-1970)	1,130

NEW YORK

CATEGORY	NAME (YEARS WITH TEAM)	TOTAL
Rushing yards	Curtis Martin (1998-2004)	8,473
Passing yards	Joe Namath (1965-1976)	27,057
Touchdown passes	Joe Namath (1965-1976)	170
Receptions	Don Maynard (1960-1972)	627
Touchdowns	Don Maynard (1960-1972)	88
Scoring	Pat Leahy (1974-1991)	1,470

GLOSSARY

Achilles tendon—tissue that connects the calf muscle to the heel and foot

bankrupt—out of money

debut—the first appearance of a person or thing

demolition—destruction, knocking down, destroying

franchises—another word for pro sports teams

Heisman Trophy—award given each year to the nation's best college football player

juggernaut—a powerful, unstoppable force

logo—a drawing or design used to represent a team or company

merge—to combine into one larger group

nemesis—enemy or rival

no-huddle offense—a style of playing in which the offensive team (with the ball) does not huddle up before every play; instead, the players line up and the quarterback calls the play from behind center

off-season—the time between sports seasons in which no games are played

postseason—the period after the regular NFL season in which the playoff games are held

wild card—an NFL playoff team that has not won a division title

TIME LINE

1960 AFL formed, first season for Buffalo Bills, New York Titans, and Boston Patriots

1964 Buffalo wins AFL title

1965 Buffalo wins AFL title for second year in a row

1968 New York Jets win AFL title, win Super Bowl III

1970 AFL merges with NFL

1972 Miami wins Super Bowl VII

1973 Miami wins Super Bowl VIII

1982 Miami wins AFC title and loses Super Bowl XVII

1984 Miami again wins AFC title and loses Super Bowl XIX

1990 Buffalo wins the first of four straight AFC championships; the team also loses four straight Super Bowls (XXV through XXVIII)

1996 New England wins AFC title and loses Super Bowl XXXI to Green Bay

2001 New England wins Super Bowl XXXVI

2004 The Patriots win their second consecutive Super Bowl and become just the second club in NFL history (after the Cowboys) to win three Super Bowls in a four-year span

THE AFC EAST AND THE NFL

B O O K S

The Boston Herald. Patriots Day: The New England Patriots' March to the Super Bowl Championship. Champaign, Ill.: Sports Publishing, Inc., 2002.

Buckley, James Jr. *NFL's Greatest Upsets.* New York: DK Publishing, 2000.

Buckley, James Jr., and Jerry Rice. *America's Greatest Game.* New York: Hyperion Books for Children, 1998.

DiLorenzo, J. J. *The Miami Dolphins Football Team.* Springfield, N.J.: Enslow Publishers, 1997.

O N   T H E   W E B

Visit our home page for lots of links about the AFC East:

http://www.childsworld.com/links

Note to Parents, Teachers, and Librarians: We routinely verify our Web links to make sure they are safe, active sites—so encourage your readers to check them out!

INDEX

A B O U T   T H E   A U T H O R

Bob Woods is a freelance writer in Madison, Connecticut.
During the past 20 years, his work has appeared in many
magazines, including *Sports Illustrated*. He has written books
for young readers about Barry Bonds, Shaquille O'Neal,
NASCAR history, and other sports topics.